MW01538627

Bearded Dragon

A Bearded Dragon Care Manual for Serious Owners

Susan McKay

Horizon Alternative School
5501 53rd Street
Olds, AB T4H 1J2

Copyright 2017 by <u>Susan McKay</u> - All rights reserved.

This document is geared towards providing exact and reliable information in regards to the topic and issue covered. The publication is sold with the idea that the publisher is not required to render accounting, officially permitted, or otherwise, qualified services. If advice is necessary, legal or professional, a practiced individual in the profession should be ordered.

- From a Declaration of Principles which was accepted and approved equally by a Committee of the American Bar Association and a Committee of Publishers and Associations.

In no way is it legal to reproduce, duplicate, or transmit any part of this document by either electronic means or in printed format. Recording of this publication is strictly prohibited and any storage of this document is not allowed unless with written permission from the publisher. All rights reserved.

The information provided herein is stated to be truthful and consistent, in that any liability, in terms of inattention or otherwise, by any usage or abuse of any policies, processes, or directions contained within is the solitary and utter responsibility of the recipient reader. Under no circumstances will any legal responsibility or blame be held against the publisher for any reparation, damages, or monetary loss due to the information herein, either directly or indirectly.

Respective authors own all copyrights not held by the publisher. The information herein is offered for informational purposes solely and is universal as such. The presentation of the information is without contract or any type of guarantee assurance.

The trademarks that are used are without any consent, and the publication of the trademark is without permission or backing by the trademark owner. All trademarks and brands within this book are for clarifying purposes only and are the owned by the owners themselves, not affiliated with this document.

Table of Contents

Introduction

Responsible owners need information right from the outset when thinking about owning a Bearded Dragon. The reason for this is that cost may be too expensive and the care the Bearded Dragon needs does cost money. Thus, there are several things you need to know prior to ownership as well as during ownership.

In this manual, we take a look at everything concerning care, so that if this is a pet you are thinking about getting, you will be able to refer to the manual and get all of the information you need. From day to day care to getting the right equipment, we will help you make your Bearded Dragon at home. Bear in mind, this is a specialist pet that will need specialist care. It isn't merely a decorative pet to show off to your friends.

With the right kind of care, your Bearded Dragon may be with you anywhere between 10 to 15 years and that's a lot of commitment. You may not have a great deal of choice of the type of dragon available in your area, though you will also find a section on the types in case you want to look further for the appropriate pet.

The book covers the kind of nutritional needs that a bearded dragon has as well as showing you foods that are unsuitable. You will also learn about the potential cost of looking after your bearded dragon and unless you are serious about its care, then this is perhaps not the pet for you. For parents thinking of buying a bearded dragon for a child, you need to ask yourself whether the child is aware of the care needed. Buying this book will help you to decide.

A pet is a major responsibility and when well looked after, bearded dragons can give you years of pleasure. As a pet owner and owner of two of these, I know because my bearded dragons have been an education to me and have helped to widen my knowledge of their history and what they expect of me, as a responsible pet owner.

Chapter 1 – Types of Bearded Dragon

A little history of their origin

Bearded dragons come from warmer climates. In fact, most derive from the Australian native dragon of South Eastern Australia. These dragons live in the wild and if you go back in history you will find that ownership of them as pets in the US and other parts of the world did not become popular until the end of the last century. Looking very similar to our idea of a dinosaur, but being very gentle in their nature, it's hardly surprising that these creatures have captured the affection of many owners over the years. For those wanting to have a low maintenance pet that is different, a bearded dragon is perfect! This is the case because their lifespan is reasonably long, for a household, they are not vicious in nature and relatively easy to look after.

The nicest feature of the bearded dragons is their bodily movements and humans can recognize their wave and find it very appealing. Used in the wild to let other creatures know that they were no threat, this wave or movement of the hand is certainly attractive and gives the dragon a character all of its own, which is what pet lovers seek in their chosen animal.

German Bearded Dragons

These are quite different in looks and less sleek than their counterparts. Typically, sandy in color, the belly area of the dragon is larger than other breeds, also I must say that their color is amazing!

The breeders of German Bearded Dragons have managed to make the breed 50 percent larger than the average bearded dragon. Because of their larger size, these dragons often go under the name "German Giant Bearded Dragons". The color range is also of interest to breeders since unique colors can be bred.

Leatherback Bearded Dragons

As you can imagine, the back on this dragon does appear to look a little like worn leather, though the color is varied. The general overview of this breed is that the scales are smaller and this makes the dragon feel nicer to stroke with your hand.

Red Bearded Dragons

There are three types of red bearded dragons and the color depends very much upon the breeding practices. For example, the more the dragon's breed, the deeper the red color can become. Thus those bought from established breeders may all come in the darker shade of red known as Ruby Red, while younger breeds may come in the color of Blood Red which is slightly less deep in color or the standard red. There have been several varieties that have been bred using red bearded dragons bred with other colors. Thus the color range available is vast, resulting in orange, tangerine, citrus and other colors that are very attractive.

Yellow Bearded Dragons

Breeders will often cross these with other colors to produce a good range of colors anywhere between a bright yellow citrus color to orange.

Albino Dragons

These are less likely to be something you will find in a pet store, but the albino breed of bearded dragons is very attractive and sparklingly white. These give off a very delicate coloring.

Most of the dragons that you are able to buy from a breeder will be a variety of the colors shown above, but there is something else to bear in mind. Not only are there types and colors. There are also different species, which makes this reptile's appearance extremely individual and varied.

It may be worthwhile checking out the type of dragon because the looks vary so much. All species names being prefixed with Pogona, you need to understand the difference between the various species because this can affect the type of tank that you purchase, as dragons vary in full grown size. The Pogona Vitticeps grow up to 24 inches in length as opposed to the Henry Lawsoni which only grows to 12 inches.

Some breeds that you may find in encyclopedias may not be available as pets since many of the attractive species are rare and are not generally sold. It's a good idea to talk about the behavior traits of your chosen dragon with the pet store or breeder. This can, for example, tell you whether the dragon enjoys climbing or not. Information like this is valuable since it will give you ideas on what to buy to make the environment-friendly and as comfortable as possible for your dragon.

Chapter 2 – Things You Will Need to Purchase

If you are thinking about buying a bearded dragon, you really do need to get your head around costs. It's too late to find out after purchase that you cannot afford the proper tank and accessories that you are going to need in order to give that pet the home it deserves.

Tanks

You will need a tank and will probably be able to buy this from your breeder, who will be able to advise you on the best size. It's worth noting that an average sized tank for a bearded dragon is about 75 gallons. Since these are costly items, you can look at second-hand markets and find a tank for a much lower price (I managed to get a great bargain on Craigslist!). A nice tank can cost you anywhere between $120-300 and the lid will cost you between $30-40, so looking at second-hand options can definitely save you some money.

UV Lamps and Heat Lights

You have to remember the needs of the dragon and UV lamps are something you are going to need. Don't economize when buying these because poor quality lights can make the environment less comfortable for your pet. The bulbs that you use aren't the same as household ones and will need to be bought from a pet store. However, you may be able to get a better price buying from Amazon or eBay. Although make sure that the seller is selling them specifically for use in a tank.

The lamp or lamps help to control the temperature within the tank and allow it to heat up to the natural heat that the bearded dragon needs for comfort. If you lived in an area like I do where lizards live, you will know that basking is part of their lifestyle habits and an important one. Heat lamps are particularly important and are needed to bring the temperature of the tank up to the required 105 degrees Fahrenheit or 40.5 Celsius.

Thinking about the natural habitat of the dragon is important because you are trying to emulate that. If you have any doubt about what lamps and bulbs to buy, make sure you ask someone who is experienced with keeping bearded dragons. Lastly, you should know that good lamps cost between $20-40.

Substrate

I have known a lot of owners who have opted for sand, thinking that this is the best bet since the dragons come from desert regions. However, for home reared pets, it isn't the best because they have a tendency to swallow the sand. You should, therefore make sure that the substrate that you choose is suitable for reptiles. It may cost you more initially but it will certain save on vet visits.

Foods

The food is an important part when it comes to looking after your bearded dragon. I know owners who skimp on this and it's not worth it! Many of the insects that you find outdoors can risk the health of the bearded dragon since there are many parasites and pesticides that can enter the digestive system of your dragon. It is far safer to buy the food from your dealership.

The main staple diet for the dragon will be crickets and you can stock up with plenty from the pet store. The average bearded dragon eats around 100 crickets per week.
The best way and the most economical way is, therefore, to buy your crickets in bulk.

You will also be able to feed the dragon various leaves from the garden as long as they are picked from safe places away from the road and away from pesticides.

There is a list of foods that are suitable for your bearded dragon in the feeding section of this manual which will give you a better idea about the treats you can give your pet. That particular section of the book also tells you about all the foods to avoid feeding your dragon. This is really important to be aware of! You will also learn about the vitamins and minerals that are needed by bearded dragons in captivity.

When you work out the entire cost, talk to your parents about this before even considering talking about having a bearded dragon. If you are an adult, then you do need to be aware of the running costs and the cost of setting up the tank. That's why we have devoted this chapter to that topic so that owners take a responsible view and do not indulge themselves in buying a dragon if they cannot afford the upkeep. It's not worth it because the bearded dragon will inevitably suffer.

You will also need to shell out on food and bulk purchase is best, as well as having somewhere to store the insects. A container for these is available at pet stores and should be counted as part of the overall cost. You may also need to check the price of the vitamins needed for your pet. Calcium and Vitamin D3 powder can be given to your dragon sprinkled on the leaves of his food but be aware of the amounts and always follow the instructions on the pack.

Chapter 3 – Tank Sizes and Set Up

Before going into technical information about tanks, lights, heaters etc. I would advise new owners to have all of this explained when they buy the tank. It's a lot of information to take in at a time when you may be overly excited about having a new pet. If you are able to get a professional to help you to set up the tank, it will save you a lot of time and energy since you won't have to deal with any problems. A reliable seller should be able to advise you on all that is needed to set up the tank in a bearded dragon friendly way.

When you buy a bearded dragon, you may buy it as a baby but you do need to understand the size that the dragon can grow to. Buying a tank suitable for a baby bearded dragon differs entirely from having a size suitable for a fully grown bearded dragon. Let me show you the difference:

Baby Tank Size 20 gallon

When you have a baby dragon, you tend to use a smaller sized tank. That way you can be sure that your bearded dragon is able to locate his food. However, if you always feed by hand, then having a larger tank is not a problem. You also need to observe the baby and ensure that the food you are giving the baby is small enough for the bearded dragon to eat. Thus, it's up to you whether you want to start with a tank this small.

12-16 inch   Tank Size 40 gallon

Although you can trade upward and get a larger tank later, I found that my baby bearded dragon was happier in a larger tank, provided that there was enough of interest in the tank. A place where the dragon could bask safely also seemed to affect my dragon's mood. This can be created by the use of suitable rocks, especially if you know that your bearded dragon loves to climb.

17-20 inch   Tank size 50-75 gallon

At this age, your bearded dragon needs to move around and a small tank prohibits this. A 50-gallon tank can be okay for a fully grown bearded dragon unless your dragon is bigger than 20 inches if so, you should opt for the 75-gallon tank.

Lighting and Humidity

What you are trying to emulate is the atmosphere that would be present in the natural habitat of the bearded dragon. Thus light and humidity should be perfect. A bearded dragon is going to need that strong light for up to 14 hours each day. The light should be defused over the whole area of the tank and you will find that most pet stores show you how the lighting systems achieve that. Furthermore, the bearded dragon needs to actually get as close as possible to the lamp for the required heat. A safe distance is up to 6 inches (15 cm) away, so when you set out your tank, you need to be able to add things like branches or rocks to help the bearded dragon to gain access higher up in the tank.

One important thing to think about when setting up the tank is that it must have a stable base and be set up near a power outlet. If you don't get the light right, your dragon can become seriously ill and thus, it's important not just to have light in the tank but to provide the amount of UVA and UVB needed.

The basking bulb also needs to be fitted, so make sure you make allowance for this when setting the tank up. For the basking bulb, do make sure that you buy your supplies from reptile experts because then you know that you are getting the right equipment.

Keeping the bearded dragon warm

It may not be something that you have considered, though avoid gimmicks like heated rocks or any kind of heating that comes from beneath the dragon. The reason for this is that the body of the bearded dragon is very fragile and heat should not be allowed to burn the skin.

I have two thermometers in my bearded dragon's tank because you need to remember that different temperatures in the tank are needed at all times. For example, on one side of the tank, the temperature that is ideal is around 100 degrees Fahrenheit (38 °C), while the cooler side of the tank is normalized around 84 degrees Fahrenheit (29 °C).

Low Humidity

Since bearded dragons need a low humidity environment, having a humidity meter is a must. The idea of having a screen top as opposed to a solid one is to allow the passage of air and this should cause no humidity at all. However, that really depends upon the environment in which you live, so you should position your tank where lower readings of humidity are obtained.

Chapter 4 – Setting Up the Environment for Your Bearded Dragon

There are all kinds of things that you can introduce to the environment that will make your bearded dragon feel right at home.

Tank backgrounds

Just like you feel comfortable in your own home, your bearded dragon also needs to feel at home and there are some pretty amazing reptile backgrounds that you can buy for your tank. These look like the desert environment in which your bearded dragon would feel right at home. These, if you buy good quality, are tear resistant. You do not need to worry about this since you can buy the exact size your tank needs and then simply tape it on the outside of the tank against a wall, so it's unlikely to cause any damage or problems. If you look on Amazon.com there are companies who sell these to size and allow you to choose the image.

Basking Platform

In the warmer side of your tank, you will need a basking platform of some kind and although natural branches can be used you need to a bit wary about what type of wood you use since it can have splinters. It's better to buy a rea lymade one because you know that it is made of safe materia s that will not harm your bearded dragon. Before buying or e, you need to measure the space in the tank so that you can)lace it sufficiently for the dragon to bask at about 6-8 in ches away from the heat lamp.

These come in the form of a bridge or rocks and our pet supply shop will be able to help you choose base(on the size of your tank and your envisioned set up.

A hiding place for your bearded dragon

It is important when you own any animal that th animal feels safe in the environment in which he is place 1. Thus, with reptiles, it's vital to have a place where the b earded dragon can hide if he wants to feel safe. When yo 1 consider the noise in an average home, there may be nois(s that will make your bearded dragon feel uncomfortable. P rovided that you give it the space to get away from this and fe(l safe, then you are providing what the bearded dragon need .

This is also needed for periods of hibernation or brumation" when your bearded dragon has to be asleep for p riods in excess of a couple of weeks. This is explained in a future chapter since it is important that you know what to expect from the behavior of your bearded dragon and brumation is an important part of their life cycle.

Substrate

We have already mentioned in a previous chapter that you should use substrate specifically designed for reptiles. However, you can use other things during the early stages of your bearded dragon's life. A reptile carpet is the best at this stage but you can also use newspapers, although please avoid using anything with wood chips since this can hurt your dragon. The problem here is that a young bearded dragon may eat insects off the floor and can easily swallow wood chips or particles from unsuitable flooring.

Water container

You will also need a water container, though this should be very shallow so that your bearded dragon cannot drown. Although they generally take moisture from the greenery that you give them, having this means that your pet is never without water if this is needed.

Other accessories

Have you ever heard of a bearded dragon feeling at home in a hammock? You may be surprised to learn that many adapt to the use of these hammocks supplied by pet stores. It's not an essential, but if you want to spruce up your bearded dragon's tank, then you may want to incorporate this in the basking area.

Whatever you buy to go into the tank, always be very sure that there is no sharpness that can hurt your bearded dragon because, as you should know by now, their skin is very delicate.

Chapter 5 – Handling of your Bearded Dragon

The handling of your bearded dragon is important. These are delicate creatures and you need to support them from the underbelly when you pick them up. Initially, it's a good idea to get the dragon accustomed to you slowly. There are certain things that you need to avoid and I have included these in this chapter to make your experience a more pleasurable one for both you and your pet.

The difference between handling a baby and an adult

You should always respect that the underbelly should be supported, but when you are handling a baby, it's important to support the dragon from just under the chin. This keeps your baby safe.

When lifting the bearded dragon from its tank, you need to use both hands. Initially, slide one hand under him and then use the other hand to give you additional support.

Things never to do and safety precautions

1.   Never startle your bearded dragon by trying to grab it by the limbs. This is dangerous for the animal and safe handling practice should always be performed to help to keep your bearded dragon safe.

2.   Never hold the bearded dragon so tightly that you are squeezing it.

3.   Never place the bearded dragon on a high surface where it is possible for the dragon to fall.

4.   Never leave your bearded dragon unattended when it is not safely in its tank

5.   Keep other pets away from the bearded dragon when you have it out of its tank.

6.   Keep the tank at a safe level so that cats cannot get into it

7.   Never make quick movements that may frighten the bearded dragon

8.   Never leave a bearded dragon with a small child who is unaccompanied by an adult.

9. Make sure small children keep the bearded dragon away from their mouths.

General handling tips

Make the relationship between you and your bearded dragon a progressive one. Hold your hand out and let the bearded dragon get accustomed to it. Always move the hand slowly when you go to pick it up.

Make it a point to always wash your hands after handling the bearded dragon.

There is every likelihood that you may get scratched by the bearded dragon because of its long claws. If you do become scratched, wash the wound and apply a disinfectant cream to the area.

The best type of soap to use when you handle a bearded dragon is a disinfectant soap. Have this available for anyone who touches the bearded dragon.

It is very rare that you will get bitten by a bearded dragon. If you do, make sure that you disinfect the area. It should go down after a couple of days, but if it doesn't then you need to visit your doctor.

Activities you can do with your bearded dragon

You can get a leash for your bearded dragon if you think that you may want to take it for walks. If you do this, it's better with adults, since they are better at coping with other environments. If you do this, avoid crowded places where the bearded dragon may become afraid.

Other toys may be available for playtime with your bearded dragon. Be aware that if you purchase a toy that requires water, the water should be dechlorinated using an appropriate Reptile safe product. If you want to take your bearded dragon into the garden for a swim, make sure that the water is no deeper than their knees and always respect the temperature requirement of 80 degrees Fahrenheit because they need that heat.

Chapter 6 – Nutrition

A responsible seller will give you a menu for your bearded dragon. If this doesn't happen, then you need to know what you can feed the dragon. This chapter deals with diet and nutrition which is extremely important. For starters, you need to know that it is better to buy your insects in bulk from a supplier than to try to catch insects from your home garden environment. The reason for this is that you will know the quality and will also know that these have been bred for the purpose of feeding your bearded dragon and do not have any risks associated such as pesticides or diseases. You will also need to house the insects that you buy, so do talk to your dealer about how these are housed. Since this varies so much from country to country, it's a little hard to be too specific, though generally, these will be housed in a feeder keeper, which controls the ambiance so that you can easily remove the insects when you need them to feed your bearded dragon. You can make a homemade one and there are instructions on this website which will help you to do this. This is done for large quantities of insects and is usually made from a plastic dustbin.

Size of insects

Your dragon can't eat anything that is bigger than the area between the eyes of or the dragon. If you measure that area it will work as a handy measurement to have, when deciding what insects to buy. These come in various sizes from pinhead (which is about the size of an ant) to one-inch crickets.

The diet of a bearded dragon varies according to age:

Baby bearded dragon: 8-12 bugs and 1 salad daily (made up of approved vegetables)
1-year-old and older: 5-10 bugs a day plus a daily salad.

Remember that older bearded dragons are less active and thus need less food. The types of foods that should be included in the feeds are as follows:

- Crickets
- Dubai Roaches
- Wax Worms
- Phoenix Worms
- Hornworms
- Super worms
- Black soldier fly Larvae
- Locusts

You will find all the details of what's available for your bearded dragon by asking at your pet suppliers. You will also need to feed your insects so that they provide the best nutrition to your bearded dragon.

The salads can be made up from the following fruit and vegetables:

Vegetables

Vegetables that are permitted are shown here:

Acorn Squash, Artichoke Hearts, Raw Asparagus, Raw Bell Peppers, Bok Choy, Cabbage, Carrots, Celery, Chicory, Cucumbers, Collard Greens, Lentils, Endives, Kale, Raw Okra, Parsnips, Pumpkins, Turnip Greens, Yams, Raw Zucchini, Yellow Squash.

Do not feed your bearded dragon other vegetables without first checking to see if these are suitable as some vegetables can prove difficult for a bearded dragon, such as lettuce.

Fruit

The fruit below can be served to your bearded dragon, cut into small pieces, though do not offer your bearded dragon fruits not shown on this list, without first checking whether these are safe:

Apples, Apricots, Blackberries, Blueberries, Cherries, Cranberries, Figs, Grapes, Grapefruit, Mangos, Melons, Peaches, Nectarine, Papayas, Pears, Pineapple, Prunes, Strawberries, Watermelons, Raisins.

You need to remember the rule that a baby bearded dragon needs 80 percent bugs and 20 percent plants, while an adult needs the opposite, 80 percent plants and 20 percent bugs.

Rhubarb and Avocado are poisonous to your bearded dragon and should never be given.

Vitamins and supplements

Your bearded dragon may not have sufficient Vitamins supplied by the diet that you give him. It is therefore recommended that you purchase Herptivite multivitamins. Type in the following in your Web-browser and you will be able to buy from Amazon: amzn.to/2s57SUz
 Feeding your dragon a multivitamin will allow you to be sure about what vitamins your bearded dragon is eating, rather than risking under- or overdosing the bearded dragon on Vitamin A which could reach toxic levels.

Calcium and Vitamin D3 are also essential for your bearded dragon and this can be supplied by the use of Rep-Cal Calcium Powder.
Link: amzn.to/2rpWoch
It should be used as follows:

- Baby Dragons – A daily dose is required for bone formation.
- Juvenile Dragons – this can be served with a meal 3-4 times a week.
- Adult Dragons – Once a week with a meal

Important Note about cleanliness

Your bearded dragon will need to have water in his tank. However, you must make sure that this is changed regularly and that there are no feces left in the water. You will be misting your dragon regularly and this will supply a lot of the moisture that is required by a bearded dragon, but, as mentioned previously, the tank should always have a shallow container of water in it to help moisture levels and to ensure that the bearded dragon has water available at all times.

Important Note on Insect Storage

Sometimes these can be smelly and it is advised that you keep your storage container in a place outside of the home but the container should be portable so that you can take it into the garage on days when it is too cold or rainy. Do not forget to keep your insects fed so that they give the best nutritional value that they can to your bearded dragon.

If you are worried about the frequency of feeding, then it may be worthwhile knowing that you cannot overfeed because bearded dragons will not eat when they are not hungry. It may sound complex, but when you get into the swing of feeding your bearded dragon, you will find that you will instinctively know when the best times to feed are and you will be able to balance their nutritional needs by keeping to the percentages shown above for live diet content and vegetable content.

I think it would be irresponsible not to link you to a very interesting page which shows the kinds of leaves that can be fed to bearded dragons. If you doubt the name of the plant from which the leaves come, do not feed it to the bearded dragon. This page gives a good explanation of the nutritional value of different leaves and also shows you which are recommended for your dragon.

Link: http://www.beardeddragonlady.com/feeder-insects.html

Chapter 7 – Bearded Dragon Care

As a new owner, you won't know what to expect of your bearded dragon. That is why this section has been created, to help you to get accustomed to the behavior of your bearded dragon and to help you understand the different things you are likely to experience while bringing up a bearded dragon:

Not eating

There will be times that cause you concern as a bearded dragon owner. For instance, most pet owners expect their fully grown pets to eat on a regular basis. However, bearded dragons may not eat for days especially when they are going through shedding. This is a natural process and you will note the scales dropping and will know that the lack of appetite is normal. However, if your bearded dragon is not eating and you are concerned about it, then you should get in touch with your vet.

Claws

You may be tempted to clip the claws of your bearded dragon. Personally, I believe this is an error and done for human comfort rather than doing anything for the bearded dragon. If you find that his claws are sharp, then introduce a climbing stone into the tank because this will help him to grind those claws down naturally. If, however, the claws continue to be a problem, it's better to get a professional to take a look and to trim them. Don't try this yourself until you have been shown by the vet how to do it.

Bathing your bearded dragon

Bathing should be part of your weekly care of your bearded dragon and this is done in the following manner. The bath should be prepared, but remember that deep water is a threat to the bearded dragon. The temperature should be warm, rather than hot or cold, and the depth of the water should not be more than up to his chest. You should never leave a bearded dragon unattended while in the bath. Washing the dragon with the warm water, you simply need to pour a little water over his back, but beware. No splashing and certainly no washing of his facial area is necessary as this may do damage. Simply trickle the water down his back to help remove scales which may be coming loose. No solution is needed for this. When the bathing is over and your bearded dragon is back in his tank, clean the bath thoroughly to get rid of any feces and disinfect it so it is ready for the next time.

Your bearded dragon deserves a clean home

The tank that you use for your bearded dragon needs to be cleaned out once a week. It is a good idea to have a smaller tank that you can place the dragon into while you clean out its tank.

Although there are people who use a diluted solution of bleach and water, I prefer to use a milder detergent and wipe down all the inside of the tank and remove any feces that may have accumulated. You will have to change the substrate as well and it's a good idea to empty the tank and then remove this into a black plastic bag so it can be disposed of easily. If you have a large tank, you may need to enlist the help of someone to lift the tank. Other than that, you can use a plastic scoop and remove the substrate.

Keeping yourself germ-free

I have already told you about the habit of cleaning your hands every time that you touch your bearded dragon, but after you have washed out the cage, you really do need to be very conscious of washing your hands in a sink that is not used in the preparation of food. Make sure that you have a good disinfectant soap and that you wash your hands thoroughly. I also keep a towel that is of a specific color, so that everyone in the house knows that this is the only towel to use after handling the bearded dragon. It's best to have two since once the cage is cleaned and you have washed your hands thoroughly, this is a good time to put the towel into the wash and get out a fresh one.

The importance of keeping the temperature correct in the tank

I told you earlier about the temperatures required in the tank, both in the basking area and in the area for non-basking. It is vital that you understand why this is so important for the bearded dragon or any other type of reptile. In its natural habitat, the bearded dragon will naturally bask because the ideal temperature for him, while he basks, is somewhere between 95 and 110 degrees Fahrenheit. The warmth that you give him in the tank emulates his natural environment. They are accustomed to sitting out in the sun and part of their natural behavior is to bask. What you may notice, if the basking area produces too much heat, is that the bearded dragon will open its mouth wide. The fact is that bearded dragons do not sweat. You may be able to get rid of extra heat by sweating, but the only way that a bearded dragon can do it is to open its mouth.

If you find this happening at too regular an interval, you may find that your platform is too near to the basking light and that the temperature on this platform is too hot. If this is the case, you can lower it slightly to achieve the ideal temperature.

Brumation

You are probably aware that mammals hibernate, but if you find that your bearded dragon doesn't seem active and doesn't seem to move much, it may be entering a period of brumation. This is the reptile equivalent of hibernation and the reason it happens is that it acts as a means of protection in winter for the bearded dragon when food supplies are scarce. People expect this to happen in winter and often it doesn't happen like that. The fact is that we have only in the last 20 years brought these delicate creatures into captivity and the brumation process is built into their way of life. This doesn't happen at a young age, but during juvenile and adult periods, can happen at any time, regardless of the fact that you keep the tank at the right temperature. If you find that the bearded dragon goes into this mode, you may find its activity a little strange. For example, if you find that he is dug into the substrate in the tank, this is likely to come from his behavior in the wild. What he is searching for is the warmth of the soil and even if you are providing that warmth, your bearded dragon can go into brumation as a natural lifestyle thing, rather than because it's winter or a specific time of year or even because of temperatures. As long as you are keeping the tank as you were taught to and the temperatures are correct, observe your bearded dragon and make sure there are no signs of distress. If you believe there are, then it may be wise to ask a vet.

The other thing that dictates brumation is that the bearded dragon may be awaiting the mating season and if this is the case, he will be trying to build up energy for this important event. The signs to look out for are ones you can recognize instantly if you have a good knowledge of the character of your bearded dragon. He will not want to play, for example, and may get grouchy when you try to move him. He won't want to sit in his basking position but will prefer to sleep in the colder part of the tank. If you find this to be the case, then you may not be able to wake him from his deep sleep. Allow brumation to take its course, but do keep an eye on your bearded dragon so that you are ready to give it the food that it needs upon waking.

Misting your bearded dragon

There are arguments for and against misting. However, the arguments against are mostly voiced because people don't know when to stop – especially kids. What I need to explain here is that it's different from bathing. Bathing allows the bearded dragon to get valuable hydration. However, misting can help in the same way as well as helping him to have sufficient water in his diet. If you are going to provide your dragon with leaves, then misting these is helpful because the bearded dragon does need a certain amount of water in the diet and is not very gifted at recognizing water in his tank as being drinking water.

If you think of it in this way, you will also know that the only water the bearded dragon needs that is extra comes in the form of gentle misting. You should never make the tank environment wet and that's the mistake that kids make. Occasionally, after basking, you can mist the face of the dragon with a very gentle mister and you will soon find out if your bearded dragon likes it. I have one that does and one that does not. Go with your gut feeling having tried gentle misting. You don't have to do this too often, but gentle misting on the facial area allows him to get a little more drinking water. Then you can place the bearded dragon into a safe tray and gently mist the back while he is shedding as this helps to hydrate the dragon and help him to shed. However, if you are bathing the dragon once a week, this isn't strictly necessary. I know with one of mine that he particularly enjoys it and I tend to spray him less than the other.

Treats for your bearded dragon

We all know that treats are wonderful. For a human being typical treats are sweet. However, for a bearded dragon, you need to keep within the parameters of safe food. Since you are not really sure what your bearded dragon likes when you first get him, introduce different fruits from the approved list shown earlier in the book before trying to experiment with foods that may be unsuitable. One of the foods that my bearded dragons love is watermelon and I guess this is a hydrating food that helps them to regulate their temperature. Cut into small pieces, I tend to leave the pips out and just give them the flesh of the fruit and they love this.

Another treat you can safely try in small amounts is scrambled egg but don't add extra things like milk. You just need to scramble the eggs together in a bowl and then microwave them, whipping them up so that they form lovely scrambled eggs. This can be kept in the fridge and you should only feed a little to your bearded dragon as a treat and make sure that it is luke-warm or cold at the time of serving.

When you do add treats remember that your dragons love the foods that they naturally consume and the richer the better. A tasty hornworm may be just as tasty to the dragon as anything new that you introduce. Never experiment with foods that you have not first checked with an authoritative website as this can be dangerous for your bearded dragon.

Conclusion

It is hoped that you have sufficient information in this book to be able to take care of your bearded dragon. However, as you get used to owning one of these precious creatures, you will get to know the character of the dragon. Owners get very close to them indeed and will usually recognize different traits that are particular to their bearded dragons.

If you are going to introduce new food, always check that it is nutritionally wise for your dragon to eat. The link that I gave you earlier on in the book will give you a guide and this is updated all the time as and when people ask questions about different plants and foods. It's a good idea to remember that this isn't just any creature that you can try hit and miss with. It's a very special creature that needs loving care and your idea of loving care and their idea of good nutrition may be very different.

The cleanliness of your hands after you have handled your bearded dragon is important. It is also important that you keep the tank clean. I would advise that keeping bearded dragons does take a lot of work and that if you believe that the work is too much for you, it's not a good idea to become an owner.

24840414R00026

Made in the USA
Columbia, SC
27 August 2018